The Sustaining Power of a Seeking Heart

How to walk more intimately with Jesus

Printed By

Accent Digital Publishing, Inc
2932 Churn Creek Rd
Redding, CA 96003
accentdigitalpublishing.com

© 2008 Kim and Mary Andersson

ISBN 978-1-60445-020-0

Christ the Rock
Publications

P.O. Box 1474, Anderson, CA 96007

Drinking from a spiritual rock... and the Rock is Christ

For Worldwide Distribution, Printed in the U.S.A.

The Sustaining Power of a Seeking Heart

How to walk more intimately with Jesus

by Kim and Mary Andersson

(Kimmary)

Christ the Rock
Publications

Dedication

This book is fondly dedicated to the memory of Eridard Mukasa. Thanks Eridard, for the profound investment in our lives and ministry at a strategic, God moment in our lives. We are more convinced than ever that there are no accidental meetings in the Kingdom, and we are still partnering with you for Kingdom purposes here on Earth. As you're rejoicing amidst the cloud of witnesses, know that your labors here have left a legacy...the seeds sown in the Secret Place. The harvest continues on. You are missed greatly by your friends and family.

Contents

Dear Seeker,

Years ago we coined the term *"Kimmary"* to describe our one-flesh form of ministry. We decided to write this book as one person, so the reader wouldn't have to keep switching back and forth between styles or characters. In a few cases you will find indications of individual thought or testimonies where we felt it would help to bring clarity to the reader. This is our personal journey into the life of intimacy with Jesus, and it is our hope that you will be encouraged to run hard after Jesus as a result of our testimony. One thing that is always a by-product of intimacy with the Lord is increased intimacy with others who are in fellowship with Christ. This is especially true of those who are privileged to be married to a spouse who is likewise passionately in love with Jesus. However, whether married or not, we think that you will find that passion for Jesus always promotes passion for His precious bride. May you become not only a more intense God lover, but also a passion filled lover of His Bride as well!

The Apostle John was once known by the nickname "Son of Thunder." However, he became utterly transformed as he spent intimate time with Jesus, learning to lean on Him and to become His best friend. In his later years he had changed so entirely, that his friends gave him a new name, "John the Beloved" or "The Apostle of Love." The metamorphosis that occurs in our lives as we commune with Christ is astounding, and John was no exception in his day. He went from being an impatient, judgmental and self-promoting disciple; to one who was consumed with passion for the maturity and growth of Christ's Body. Initially, there seemed to be no end to his impetuous and passionate nature; from arguing about who was the greatest, to asking if he could have a throne next to Jesus in Heaven, to calling down the wrath of God on an entire city. So, what eventually changed his character? We believe that it was as he turned His passion and competitive nature toward the pursuit of becoming "God's favorite kid," that he learned instead, to become a lover. The outflow of his love life for God was love for God's children. He learned the secret that the two were inseparable. There is actually only one legitimate form of greed that is allowed in our Christian walk...that is the passionate resolution to pursue friendship with God and the life of the Spirit. May your heart become inflamed, and may your eyes ravage the heart of the Lord with just one glance!

With much love, Kimmary

Introduction

So what exactly is this "power" that we can receive in the "secret place," and what do we mean when we promise to show you how to have "a more intimate walk with Jesus?" It's a familiar spiritual journey that was once well known by many of the ancient Christian mystics, such as Brother Lawrence and Teresa of Avila; but unfortunately it's become a lost practice among most western believers over the last several centuries. Fortunately for us, it is a well traveled pathway that many in our day are beginning to rediscover, as they pursue a deeper relationship with the Lord. This type of prayer/lifestyle is known by a number of names; i.e. to "tabernacle" with the Lord, to "practice the presence," "listening prayer," to be "overshadowed" by the Lord, "intimate prayer," "to tarry" or to "wait on the Lord." However, it is probably more easily understood by most as "soaking prayer." The analogy is both clear and direct... although certainly not a complete picture. As a launching place, begin by picturing for a moment, a dry sponge, which you have placed under a dripping faucet. After a long while, it will reach the saturation point where it is no longer just sucking in the water, but it begins to seep out, or leak. If you keep that sponge under a steady supply of water, it doesn't ever have to become dry and shriveled again. As we rest under the anointing, then we become just like that sponge...we become increasingly full of the Spirit, until He just oozes out of us! This is what it is like to simply "wait on the Lord." We wait...He comes...we become saturated with His presence. This actually may be referred to as "Seeking 101"... the starting place. We will endeavor in the pages to come to show you the pathway that will cause you to plumb the depths of God, climb Jacob's ladder, and pull down the anointing on a regular basis.

Chapter one

Made to Relate
Fellowship

The truth is we were created for fellowship with the Lord. God's original design, as shown in the book of Genesis, was for man to walk with the Lord in daily communion. *"And they heard the voice of the Lord God walking in the garden in the cool of the day...And the Lord God called to Adam and said, 'Where are you?'"* (Genesis 3:8-9) God was used to talking with Adam, and He expected him to show up at the usual time to meet with Him! They probably even had a favorite spot in the garden. When Adam didn't show up for their date, on that fateful day that he chose to hide from God's face... the Lord began to call out to him, "Where are you?" This is the same call that tugs on *our* hearts today. You see, the Lord has never stopped longing to fellowship with us, His beloved creation.

II Corinthians 13:14 encourages us with this prayer, *"May the...fellowship of the Holy Spirit be with you all!"* The word for "fellowship" in the original Greek is the word "koinonia." It means communication, partnership or (social) intercourse. The word implies intimacy...the kind you would share with a close friend. Another definition for the word fellowship is distribution. The truth is, we are given precious gifts by the Holy Spirit, and it is His good pleasure for them to be "distributed" to the Body of Christ. This is an important feature of fellowshipping with the Lord. He fills us, He communicates with us... and as an added blessing, when He comes to spend time with us, He brings gifts that will bless others! I Corinthians 12:11 says, *"But the one and the same Spirit, supernaturally works all these things distributing to each, just as He intends."* There's that word again! When we spend time with the Lord, He delivers His abundant supplies to us, and then we in turn, become His "distribution" center!

Abide in Me

It is so important that as we walk with Christ, we manifest His presence wherever we go, who *"... through us (manifests) diffuses the fragrance of His knowledge in every place. For we are to God the fragrance of Christ..."* (II Corinthians 2:14-15) It is absolutely crucial to understand that we are not only "distributing" His gifts as was just mentioned, but we are also "distributing" His fruit. Otherwise, we really are... "nothing." (See I Corinthians 13:2)

Most of us are painfully aware, that the fruit of the Holy Spirit should consistently flow out of us like a river, "...*love, joy, peace, longsuffering, kindness, goodness, faithfulness, gentleness, self-control.*" (Galatians 5:22-23) It's certainly a familiar truth, yet, not always present in the life of the believer...Why?

Well, the secret is hidden in the phrase "fruit of the Spirit." Sometimes I think we forget that WE don't produce the fruit...we "MANIFEST" the fruit. This implies the need for connectedness. If we desire the continual yield of the Spirit, both fruit and gifts, we must remain in communion with the Lord. I asked the Lord this morning after spending a glorious time in His presence, "What would You like to show me in Your Word today?" He had me turn to the book of Hosea, where I read in chapter 14:8, *"...Your fruit is found in Me."* Simple to be sure, but powerful and profound! The word "found" means **to be present.** We must be PRESENT IN HIS PRESENCE, if we wish to manifest His fruit. Jesus made this truth abundantly clear when He told His disciples in John 15:4-5, *"Abide in Me, and I in you. As the branch cannot bear fruit of itself, unless it abides in the vine, neither can you,*

15

unless you abide in Me. I am the vine, you are the branches. He who abides in Me, and I in him, bears much fruit; for without Me you can do nothing." The word "abide" means **to stay (in a given place, state, relation or expectancy)**. It also means...you guessed it...to **be present**!

It is true, that if you cut off a fruit laden branch from a tree, and stick it in a bucket of water, it will live...for a time. It's also a fact that Christmas trees kept in water after being cut down, certainly manage to survive in our homes for a whole month while we celebrate the holidays. However, it is certainly not their place of thriving. True growth comes from being rooted in. We must practice His presence continually, if we wish to manifest true life in Christ. The secret of His life and power is found as we learn to abide in the vine.

Friend of God

We have a great example in the Old Testament of a man who spent time everyday in God's presence. He even built a special place to meet with God called the "tent of meeting." His nickname was "Friend of God." Wouldn't that be a great name to be known by for all eternity? Several wonderful facts are recorded in Scripture about the man called Moses, which reflect the benefits of regularly spending time enjoying the Lord:

16

1. Moses had a very intimate relationship with the Lord. Numbers 12:8 says, *"He sees Me face to face, and everything I say to him is perfectly clear."* CEV Moses heard God's voice, and we can too. Jesus declared to His disciples that His followers would know His voice. John 10:2 says *"...The sheep know their shepherd's voice. He calls each of them by name and leads them out."* CEV

2. Moses knew God's heart. He understood the desires of the Lord, and he even understood how to change God's heart. "He made known His ways to Moses, His acts to the children of Israel." (Psalm 103:7) The word "ways" means **a road (as trodden),** or a mode of life, or course of action. In other words, when you walk intimately with someone, their ways become like a familiar road to you, and you understand what course of action they will take. If you're close enough, you might even be able to change their mind about a course of action they're planning to take. Moses often did this when God was angry with the children of Israel! There were many occasions where Moses begged God not to wipe them out, and because of His friendship with Moses, God relented.

3. Moses was utterly changed in the presence of the Lord. Even his physical appearance changed as he spent time with God. The glory of God was on him in such a profound way, that he had to wear a veil over his face. *"...The sons of Israel were not able to look upon the face of Moses, because of the glory of his face...how will the ministry of the Spirit (in us today) not be more glorious?"* (II Corinthians 3:7-8)

Moses' countenance was changed, and so will ours be changed. We can look forward to an even greater expression of the Holy Spirit today. These are the same benefits we can enjoy, and more, as we spend time with Jesus! God's glory will manifest in our lives.

4. Moses had a young disciple who always followed after him into the tent of meeting. His name was Joshua. In Exodus 33:11 we read that, *"The Lord spoke to Moses face to face as a man speaks to his friend. He returned to the camp, but his servant, Joshua...departed not out of the tent."* Joshua's character was also being changed in the presence of the Lord. We can see for this young man, that the fruit of spending regular time in God's presence, was a life full of faith and "God can do" thinking. He was among the spies that were sent out by Moses to spy out the land that God had promised them. After taking one look at the land with his friend Caleb, they declared that there were giants in the land, but that the land was "flowing with milk and honey" and was worth taking.

The other spies, after declaring that there were giants in the land said, *"...we were in our own sight as*

18

grasshoppers, and so we were in theirs." These spies were not looking at the situation from God's vantage point, because they had not been spending time in God's presence the way Joshua had. They had not gained "God can do" thinking! When we spend time in God's presence, we will loose our own "grasshopper" mentality. The real truth is hidden in the book of Isaiah 40:22-26. *"All the inhabitants of the earth are like grasshoppers in the eyes of the Lord; He brings princes (and giants!) to nothing, and none (of His own) fails!"* If we hide ourselves in Him regularly, we will know this deep in our spirit, and be able to stand strong when the enemy comes.

Chapter two

Obtaining Vision
Increased Vision

Probably one of the greatest benefits we receive whenever we wait on the Lord is a renewed strength and sense of purpose or vision. Let's look closely at a very familiar passage in the book of Isaiah. Isaiah 40: 27-31 says, *"Why do you say Jacob, and speak Israel, 'My way is hidden from the Lord, and my judgment is passed over from my God? Have you not known? Have you not heard, that the everlasting God, the Lord, the Creator of the ends of the earth, doesn't faint and isn't weary? There is no lack of His understanding. He gives power to the faint; and to those that have no might He increases strength. Even youths faint and grow weary, and young men utterly fall. But, those who wait upon the Lord shall renew their strength; they shall mount up with wings as eagles; they shall run, and not be weary; and they shall walk, and not faint."*

This is an interesting passage. Note that it begins with God's people having a distorted mind set. This deception, or distortion of thinking, could have begun with the difficulties in their lives described in verse 24. Apparently, there were issues and hardships in their lives that brought on these conditions within their heart; they were not firmly "planted," they were not "sown," they had not taken "root," they were "withered," and left with nothing but "stubble" to be blown away. It was not a pretty picture! Hard times were abundant, and they had become weary. Difficulties always tend to reveal what we're made of. They can show us how deeply rooted we are in God, and whether or not we're a fruitful field or just filled with stubble.

Unfortunately, weariness is a powerful foe, as it can easily lead to distorted thinking. So, they began to believe a lie...that their *"way (was) hidden from the Lord"* and that they were not receiving the justice that was due them. But the truth that they seemed to have forgotten is that the Lord is never lacking in *"understanding."* This is the Lord who is referred to in Scripture as the one who *"never slumbers...and never sleeps."* He had not overlooked them; they had overlooked Him! He was their answer, and He is our answer. He is the only one who can provide us with "power" and "might" to overcome *if* we will spend time seeking Him.

This plight knows no boundaries. Young and old alike are susceptible to losing their vision and their strength. No one is immune to this attack. There is a grave danger in becoming weary. Just take a look at Esau who lost his birthright when he grew weary. He gave it up for a lousy crust of bread and some stew! When we are weary, we can easily lose sight of our vision. Proverbs 29:18 says, *"Where there is no vision, the people perish . . . "* The word "perish" means **to be naked**. It is the same word used to describe the children of Israel when they were dancing in a wild frenzy around the golden calf! Vision is important to have and to keep. It must constantly be renewed, so that it remains fresh. We used to sing a song many years ago by an unknown author that proclaimed, "For without a progressive vision, you'll dwell carelessly. So lift your vision higher, and you will see the glory of the Lord!" There is only one dependable means to accomplish this, and that is to soar with the Lord on "wings of eagles," as we wait on His presence.

David, the young shepherd, understood this truth well. After much time spent in the field with the flocks...no doubt meditating and basking in the Lord's presence...he had obviously gained a different viewpoint of the enemy than his brothers. As he came to drop off lunch one day, his perspective became obvious when he made the bold proclamation about Goliath, *"Who is this uncircumcised Philistine, that he should taunt the living armies of the living God?"* (I Samuel 17:26b NAS) He had come to know, through experiencing God's greatness, that the same King of the Universe who had helped him take down a lion and a bear, would also be there to help him defeat a mocking, cursing giant. David's entire victory over Goliath was indicative of his faith grid, developed in the presence of the Lord. Our take on the obstacles of life changes for us too, as we abide regularly in fellowship with our God. (See I Samuel 17:4-51)

Bound together

The words "to wait" mean to bind together or to expect. When we patiently wait for Him, He WILL come and meet with us. The promise is clear...when He comes, He will renew our strength. The word "strength" in this passage is truly multifaceted. It means...**firm, vigor, force, capacity, means, produce, hardiness, power, might, substance and wealth!** Wow, what benefits! The rewards for waiting on the Lord are phenomenal, and almost without measure. If that weren't enough to entice us, the Lord also promises that we will be able to run without growing weary and walk without fainting. The word "faint" means **to tire (as if from wearisome flight)**. This seems to be a picture of someone who is being hunted down or pursued, yet does not lose their strength. So, if we practice the presence of the Lord, even our enemies will not be able to wear us down! The Lord is inviting you to a lifestyle that is full of benefits.

Many Christians today desire to walk in a power anointing, yet they are not willing to be plugged into the power source long enough to get their spiritual batteries recharged. This is a particularly important truth for ministers and future ministers to understand. There are certain power expenditures in ministry that will actually drain virtue from you . . . Jesus mentions "virtue" going out of Him when the woman with the issue of blood touched the edge of his robe. (See Mark 5:30) The word "virtue" is the Greek word **dunamis,** from which we derive the word dynamite. When we minister in the Holy Spirit, there is a literal spiritual explosion that occurs, that can actually shock our frail physical being. The process can be both physically, as well as emotionally taxing. Like the common household battery... we too, cannot run too long, or too hard, without a "recharge." And, there are some power usages that tend to drain our "batteries" more than others.

The Jesus Pattern

Jesus, who lived life as a man when He was here walking the earth, regularly spent time fellowshipping with His Heavenly Father. He set an example for us to follow. If Jesus needed to spend a lot of time with God, then so should we. Here are some of the Biblical accounts that present this lifestyle to us as an example:

"When Jesus therefore perceived that they would come and take Him by force, to make Him a king, He departed again to the mountain Himself alone." (John 6:15)

"...Jesus...went...to a place where there was a garden...He often met there..." (John 18:1-2)

"...They went up on a very high mountain where they could be alone. There in front of the disciples, Jesus was completely changed. His face was shining like the son, and His clothes became white as light." (Matthew 17:1-2)

"And it came to pass in those days, that he went out into a mountain to pray, and continued all night in prayer to God." (Luke 6:12)

"...as He was praying in a certain place, when he ceased, one of His disciples said to Him, 'Lord, teach us to pray...'" (Luke 11:1)

"When Jesus heard this, he went by boat to a deserted place by Himself." (Matthew 14:13)

"Then Jesus was led by the Spirit into the wilderness...he had fasted forty days..."

(Matthew 4:1-2)

As we read these examples of Jesus prayer life we can see a number of reasons that He practiced this intimate lifestyle.   Look at the reasons listed below that Jesus used to promote this type of prayer life:

He went away to spend time with His Father before He began His ministry.

He went away to spend time with His Father before affecting great miracles.

He went away to spend time with His Father after affecting great miracles.

He went away to spend time with His Father after great loss in His life.

He went away to spend time with His Father before facing great temptation.

He went away to spend time with His Father before His crucifixion.

He went away to spend time with His Father before making decisions.

He went away to spend time with His Father when He was fatigued.

He went away to spend time with His Father and became "transfigured."

He went away to spend time with His Father to

learn His will.

He went away to spend time with His Father so He could receive instruction.

He went away to spend time with His Father... OFTEN.

Taste and See

Some of you may be wondering why you can't just spend this kind of time with God when you're at church. You may be thinking, "After all, the anointing is so strong in our meetings, and I feel so close to God when I'm there. The worship helps me to focus, and with everyone doing the same thing together, I'm able to concentrate a whole lot better!" Well, it is wonderful to experience the corporate anointing when God's people gather together, but if this is the only time you really "enter into the Presence," then you are truly missing a treat. It's a little like going to the mega-store, Costco, and taking a sample from each of the demo people, without ever purchasing the product and taking it home! The demo people are paid by the manufacturers to demonstrate their products. The samples are meant to entice you to purchase the product and take it home to enjoy. They are hoping, in fact, that you will become a regular customer. If you never ever buy the product, then you are missing the point. That is not the vision, or heart of the manufacturer!

At Costco, on any given weekend, you can, amidst the crowds of shoppers, notice a handful of pretend shoppers shuffling along with empty grocery carts in front of them (you would think they'd be smart enough to throw a few items in their cart so as not to be so easily identified). These are what are known in the industry as "tasters" or the "lunch crowd." They have discovered a clever way to enjoy their lunch "on the house," several times a week. They've found that they can save 20-30 dollars on meals each week by nibbling their way through the store. They have their card that entitles them to membership, but they NEVER, EVER, take the product home! This is like a lot of "card carrying" church attendees that we know.

The Bible says, *"Oh taste and see that the Lord is good!"* (Psalm 34:8) Why do you suppose the psalmist instructs us to "taste" and then to "see?" Shouldn't he be telling us to "look" and then to "see?" Well, the word "taste" means **to perceive**. And, Webster's Dictionary defines the word perceive this way, "to comprehend, to take, to have or obtain knowledge or awareness of by the senses." Perceiving the Lord's goodness will change the way we look at things in the world around us. Our natural sense of taste will produce memories that last a lifetime. You can probably remember vividly, the worst, as well as the best thing you ever tasted! Both experiences have created an indelible impression in your mind that won't soon be forgotten. It is like this with whatever we "taste" in the spirit realm too. Then, we are told by the psalmist to "see" His goodness. The word "see" in this passage means **(make to) enjoy, have experience, visions,** and it also means **to spy.** Remember how the spy, Joshua, was able to have proper vision about the Promised Land because of all the time He spent experiencing God in the tent of meeting? Where do you think he originally received his incredible insight and visionary way of thinking? It is essential for us to experience God first hand, or we will never have a testimony of our own. We too, need to learn how to spy out the land of our inheritance from a heavenly vantage point. We need to see things from God's perspective first. How does He view our situation?

It is only by first hand experience that we can declare with faith that God is good all the time, and all the time, God is good! Experiences we have in God create testimonies that produce other testimonies, which produce other testimonies, which produce even more testimonies. The Lord truly desires to commune with you regularly and open up the eyes of your heart. *"...No eye has seen, no ear has heard, no mind has imagined the things that God has prepared for those who love Him. But God has revealed those things to us by His Spirit. For the Spirit searches everything,*

even the deep things of God." (I Corinthians 2:9-10)
We can expect the Lord to speak to us about His
mysteries. After all, friends tell friends secrets.

It is important and strengthening for us to
experience God in the corporate anointing. God visits
His people powerfully as we gather together. Jesus
prayed that we would be one as He and the Father are
one. Psalm 133 declares that it is "good" and
"pleasant" for brothers to "dwell in unity." Verse 3
says that it is a place of "commanded blessing." We
are also told in Scripture that wherever two or three
are gathered together in "His Name," that He would be
"in their midst." David declared he was "glad"
whenever anyone said "let's go up to the house of the
Lord." The Lord definitely responds whenever His
people come together to seek His face. Having said
this, we will truly maximize our corporate experience
by spending frequent quality time alone with the Lord.
What we have personally experienced in God's
presence, is what we will bring with us when we gather
with God's people. Trying to hear from God only when
you're in a meeting, is a bit like trying to converse with
a friend at a party. You'll only catch bits and snatches
of the conversation. To hear your friend's heart, you
must spend time alone together.

Secrets are for Friends

Is it true that the Lord wishes to tell you His secrets? Of course He does.

Scripture tells us that *"It is the glory of God to conceal a thing: but it is the glory of kings to search out a matter."* (Proverbs 25:2) The Bible identifies us as the "priests" and the "kings." The prophet, Daniel, expected God to reveal His secrets to him. He actually referred to God as "the One who reveals secrets." Psalm 25:14 even tells us, *"The secrets (intimacy) of the Lord, are for those who fear (revere) Him..."* We need to expect the same thing from God. Often times, we have not, because we ask not. It's time to start seeking, asking and knocking. Remember, friends tell friends their secrets. So, it's time to become better friends with God.

Chapter three

Testimonies

Frustration is not your Portion

OK, so hopefully you're convinced by now that God really wants to spend time with you, and that it is a beneficial path to follow...this path of intimacy. You may be asking, "But, how do I get started?" "I've tried to rest in His presence before, and after five minutes, I'm checking my watch and counting the tiles on the floor, or creating pictures in my mind with the dots on the ceiling...Help!" Well, let's begin by sharing with you our personal road of discovering the depths of God's presence. Then, we'll cover some practical helps toward bringing our souls (mind, will and emotions) into subjection to our spirit man, so the Holy Spirit can bring us into the Lord's presence.

For both of us, the pathway to greater intimacy

began with first recognizing the lack in our lives. Many years ago, we were frustrated with our then, fledgling ministry, and unfortunately already had a track record of frustration, having experienced spiritual burnout with a prior investment in ministry that had failed during the early years of our marriage. I remember all those years ago that a prophet visited our church and told us that "frustration was not our portion," and sadly, we found that word to be just plain, well... frustrating! We were deeply concerned that we would not repeat the past. So, we had entered into a time of fasting from food, but also from entertainment. This is an important point to note, in that God responds to spiritual hunger. Often, it's necessary to lay aside the spiritual idols in our lives in order to produce a greater hunger for the things of the Lord. We had also been studying the revivals of old, and the testimonies we read about had fueled a desire for more of the Lord in our personal lives and ministry. This is another point to remember... other's testimonies can help to fan our own desire, and point to the necessary pathway to follow.

During that season, the Lord arranged for us to meet a young Ugandan revivalist who was living in the LA area, at a conference we happened to be attending. We sensed such a strong anointing in his life, and when he began to share with us about the revival going on in Uganda, we realized that this was a current day testimony of the revivals of old we had been reading about! He was used to preaching at crusades of up to 70,000, and although we did not have the means to host meetings of any real substance, we took a chance and we invited him up to visit us. With a brand new congregation of less than twenty people, we realized that all we really had to offer to him was a sense of family. That was all that was in our hands at the moment, so we offered what we had! We wrote a simple letter offering our friendship, and an invite to stay with us anytime he was passing through our area.

Much to our surprise, he responded right away and came up to see us at his own expense. We planned a few meetings with only mild success as far as attendance goes, but the anointing was greater than anything we had experienced to date. He carried with him such a strong presence of the Lord! People would fall out under the anointing when he would simply pass by. His wisdom and revelatory capacity held us captivated, so that we would stay up till the wee hours of the morning each night hanging on to every word he shared with us. Signs and wonders were an every day reality for him. We quickly arranged with other ministers in our region for our new friend to minister in a number of the area churches. He cleared much of his speaking schedule elsewhere in order to remain with us for three and a-half weeks, and by the time he left our region; he had spoken to thousands of people. The blessing for us was that during this time, he remained in our home and continued to share his heart of intimacy with us. We were so hungry that we gladly gobbled up all he had to throw our way. He had so many testimonies of the dead being raised and blind eyes being opened; and we were also seeing many miracles first hand. This was the life of the Spirit we had always longed for.

So why was this man so different? Well, from the first night he stayed in our home, we definitely knew something was out of the ordinary. We fixed breakfast for him, and that came and went without his appearance outside the bedroom we had him staying in. Then, lunchtime came and went, and still... no sign of our friend, Eridard! At this point we were getting a little worried, so we sent our youngest daughter to crawl into the closet of the bedroom next door to his. We told her to put an ear against the wall and tell us whether she could hear any noise. In the back of our minds, we were actually starting to wonder if he had passed away during the night! We asked her what she heard, and she replied that all she could hear was what sounded like a Rain Bird sprinkler and the occasional mention of the names of our family. Ahhhh, it finally dawned on us...he was praying in the Spirit...for hours on end apparently! But, how could someone pray for hours on end without a break, we wondered? It was now nearly three o'clock in the afternoon! He had become so lost in the presence of the Lord, that time had no meaning or pull on him. We witnessed over the three week period he was in our home, that this was his regular practice.

As we stayed up late, after every meeting, chatting with him; he began to share the secret of his strong anointing. It was held up, behind closed doors, in the place of complete communion and abiding with the Lord. As he spent many hours waiting on the Lord, he was literally being "clothed with power from on high," just like the early disciples had been! (See Luke 24:49) But, how was he able to remain in the Presence so long, we questioned? There were many helpful tools he shared with us, which we will share with you as well... plus some we've discovered on our own pathway toward intimacy. But, first we'll share the rest of our personal testimony of discovering the way into His presence.

Mary's Testimony

I was excited and depressed all at the same time as I listened to Eridard's testimony. I was fully convinced it was the right path, yet felt utterly helpless to apply this new truth to my own life. At this stage of life, I was a young mother, with four children that I home-schooled, and a brand new and very needy church. Our marriage and ministry was a joint effort, so I was fully engaged in every aspect of church life. How in the world was I going to find extra time to spend in the presence of the Lord, beyond my morning devotions that I already barely had time for? Good grief, I actually kept my Bible in the bathroom during those days, so I could read it without interruption! I was in desperate need of a stronger anointing in my life, but felt utterly helpless that I could ever really achieve it. I wept with frustration.

Eridard actually took a day alone with Kim, where he showed my husband how to break through into the Lord's presence. Then, Kim described to me what the process looked like. At the end of the three weeks, after Eridard left for home, I was left alone to discover my own pathway to intimacy. My husband and I started, on a regular basis, to take large blocks of time, while the children napped, to wait on the Lord together in the sanctuary of our church. This was a fruitful effort, but I still needed to discover my own path. I gave it a lot of thought and decided that the middle of the night was best for me and my schedule, since my waking hours were filled with people. I reasoned that I had once been able, in the course of nursing four children over the years, to wake up in the middle of the night, nurse a baby, and then go back to sleep...still managing to keep up with my day and my responsibilities. This would be no different. I would set my alarm for 3:00am, get up out of bed, go to the living room and wait on the presence of the Lord. I made a covenant with the Lord. I would give Him one month to show up... no more, no less. I would do my part, and He would have to do His. I felt so dead inside, that it really didn't matter to me that I would be missing my sleep. It was a small price to pay, if there was even a slight chance that I could become alive again.

I told the Lord, for these late night ventures, that I could not waste a lot of time trying to breakthrough into His presence. I would simply walk into the middle of the dark living room (no lights, so I wouldn't be distracted by the sudden urge to clean house!), and stand there (since sitting would probably cause me to fall back to sleep!) I wasn't exactly sure what I was waiting for, but I remembered that Eridard had explained that this was a time for just showing my love and devotion to the Lord, so I would just pray in the Spirit and softly tell Him, "I love you. I desire you. Draw me closer to you, Lord." This process went on for many days, without any seeming results, yet after a number of days, I actually began to look forward to these late night rendezvous! I didn't put a time limit on how long I would stand there, but I would try to stay focused as long as I was able. Sometimes I think it was only a mere fifteen minutes or so.

Then one night, that was really no different than

the others had been, something changed. That night, I stood in the middle of my dark living room, waiting for something to happen. Suddenly, I became aware of someone standing beside my left shoulder, just watching me...strange to be sure. No physical presence was in the room, but I realized instead, it was the Spirit of the Lord! A great fear washed over me, as I became acutely aware of my smallness and His largeness. I knew in my heart that if He wanted, He could squash me like a bug! Yet, because I was so dead inside, I was willing to risk anything for some kind of change. So, I took a chance and invited Him to come closer and to do whatever He wanted to do. He responded to my invitation, and I heard and felt a great wind rush over me. It left me breathless and weak, yet exhilarated all at the same time. It was wonderful! I begged Him to stay, but that was all I felt during that first encounter with Him. As I continued night after night in hot pursuit of the Lord, I realized that the experience was not the same every time. Sometimes I felt nothing at all, yet I knew I was somehow standing on a gold mine. I kept my part of the bargain that entire month, and the Lord kept His!

More substantial than any feeling or experience, was that I began to notice some dramatic changes in my life...less frustration for one. I guess the prophet guy, who had spoken to us all those years ago, was right after all. Frustration really wasn't my portion! I began to have an increase in dreams and even a few visions. But, what was even more fantastic, was that God was beginning to head trouble off at the pass for us. Whenever there were problems in the lives of the people we were pastoring, the Lord would give us dreams and words of revelation that would intervene in their lives. God was regularly intersecting in our everyday lives, and our joy was returning! There was real and lasting fruit in this lifestyle of intimacy! I have continued pursuing this path for 14 years now, and the only regrets I have are when I don't practice it enough or that I didn't start many, many years ago. Now that we have a target to aim at, I'm always able to tell when I haven't spent enough time with the Lord. Frustration is no longer my portion, and neither is spiritual burn out.

As time went on, I started to include other times in my schedule to be with God. These times would shift according to our schedules and family responsibilities as the years went by. For many years, I blocked out Sunday afternoons and evenings to be with the Lord. After Sunday morning service and lunch with family and friends, I would excuse myself and go to our prayer room at the church in our first facility. These were awesome and uninterrupted times in the Spirit. Then, eventually, my husband discovered a ministry about an hour or so from our house that allowed pastors to come for free a number of times per year in order to pray. They had little prayer cottages on the property. After going there for a number of months, my husband persuaded me to give it a try. I resisted at first, feeling that I shouldn't leave my responsibilities at home, but eventually succumbed to the desire to be alone with the Lord. Kim assured me that he would be happy to take over on the home front for me. I'll never forget the first morning waking up in that little prayer cottage...it was SO QUIET! As I peered out from under the covers after waking, I just started to laugh, overjoyed to be completely and utterly alone with Jesus!

We each endeavor to get away to those prayer cottages a minimum of 6 times per year. Plus, we also schedule times in hotels a few times per year (usually attached to the front end of various speaking venues in other cities), attempting to average one time away per month (not always successfully, but it remains a number one priority for us to always attempt). I will mention here, that when I go away like this, I have made a covenant with the Lord about my time with Him. The prayer cottages that we travel to are 1 hour and 10 min. from our doorstep. I have told the Lord that whatever I need to process/pray/grieve over, that I will ONLY do that during my travel time. When I arrive at the gate of the retreat center...I leave my issues at the gate.

I've made a commitment to the Lord that when I

am with Him; it is strictly honeymoon time, except for a brief period of study on the front and tail end of my stay. The time with Him is so precious, that I don't want to be distracted from His Presence with issues or personal frustrations. I have also told the Lord that if He doesn't touch me in a way that helps me to either resolve or be at peace with these issues while I'm communing with Him, then He will have to listen to me complain about these things all the way home. In 14 years of communing with the Lord in this way, I am happy to report that I have NEVER had to pick my problems back up at the gate and take them home! He either gives me answers while I'm with Him, or I become so intoxicated with His love that I no longer feel worried or stressed! My problems have minimized in the awesomeness of His glory!

Kim's Testimony

Like Mary, I was baffled over the idea of spending extra time just enjoying God's presence. I was personally in a place of true desperation... facing a possible re-entry into burnout. Yet, I believed myself to already be a praying man. It was hard to wrap my mind around what our new friend was trying to teach us regarding prayer. This revelation was coming to us at a time period when revival still seemed so far off... the stuff of history books and third world nations. It was a season when no one talked much about intimacy with the Lord. People's private prayer lives were, well... private! While we listened to our friend Eridard, I kept saying to my self, "But I do pray, I'm praying all the time." But, the type of intimate prayer Eridard was talking about was not the petitioning prayer that I was accustomed to.

Thankfully, he took some time not only to just talk with me about it, but to give me a living example of what He was talking about. We took about three hours together one afternoon, when everyone was gone from the house. We lay on the floor and worshiped and prayed in the Spirit...on and off, calling on the Lord's presence. As time went by, Eridard became more intense in his pursuit...drawing on the Spirit, and yet it was not really a sense of working something up. He was just focused and pressing on the Lord for a deeper encounter. Eventually, he seemed to reach a place of tangible breakthrough and fell quiet as he basked in God's glory. He was obviously quite comfortable and used to this place; while for me, I was still just a spectator. However, it did give me something to shoot for, and so I started my own quest to draw further into Jesus.

The main thing of course, was finding that place of solitude where there were no distractions. This was especially crucial at the start, as I was easily distracted and my ability to stay focused was limited.

So, therefore, I REALLY needed a place of quiet. I

tried at first getting up in the middle of the night like Mary did, but that didn't work for me. I don't know if I'm less dainty as I trudge through the house than her, but each time I got up in the wee hours to go into the living room...so did one of my then, small children! Before long they were on my lap and wanting a story or a heart-felt talk with Daddy. So, somewhere more secluded was going to have to fit the bill for my times alone with Jesus.

Desperate needs, call for desperate measures, which are taken by desperate men. At this particular season in our lives, too many people had keys to our church building to assure the privacy I needed. So, I had to get creative. I began to take ridiculously long drives out into the boonies. I would start heading east, past every small town with strange names, till there were no longer any signs pointing to anything. With no sign of human life, I would find a convenient place to pull off the side of the road. It was as quiet as quiet ever gets. I would begin to press past the only distractions left, which were those trapped inside my mind... and then, just as I would begin to relax and settle in, a very strange thing would happen. I may not have passed any cars at all for nearly twenty minutes during my drive time, yet just about the time I was starting to enjoy myself while sitting alone, a car would suddenly come barreling down the road. Oddly, it would begin to slow down, then to crawl along, and then for no explainable reason, other than the devil himself surely must have been behind the wheel... the car would turn off the road and the driver would park right next to me! Go figure! I even tried a variety of remote locations...I drove across to the other side of the valley...and guess what? A car would appear out of nowhere and park right next to me. It actually happened repeatedly! Yet, despite the ridiculous resistance, (when it gets this obvious, you know it's the enemy) I was undaunted in my pursuit. I was obviously on to something, and it seemed the devil was afraid I might actually discover a very important secret! That made me all the more determined in my quest.

I finally abandoned the long drive idea. However, it wasn't long before I made some adjustments on the situation of "too many people with keys" back at the church, which finally afforded me the solitude I was looking for. I staked out a spot in my office on the floor, where I placed a cushion, and set a time each day that was to be my "seek" time. I started with singing some praise and worship songs to get focused and then began to call on the Lord like Eridard had done. I remember he had told us to keep drawing on the Spirit, as though wooing His presence; then if I began to sense a change in the atmosphere, to beg the Holy Spirit to remain. It took quite some time before I got to that place. At first, it was mostly about consistency and my commitment to devote a portion of time solely to the pursuit and worship of the Lord. I noticed as I practiced, that staying focused on what I was doing became easier. There were still times when I just felt alone, surrounded only by four walls and I would begin to make patterns out of the texture on the ceiling. But, I remained resolute to my goal. Praying in tongues helped quite a bit, and as a start, I had grabbed the book, "Good Morning, Holy Spirit" by Benny Hinn to read. This helped me in the beginning, because the book is mostly about inviting the Holy Spirit to commune with you. I would draw on God, pray in tongues for a while, tell Him how much I loved Him, read some scripture, pray in tongues some more, read a little in my book...then I would kind of repeat the process again. In time the Lord honored my attempts, and I began to sense His presence. I was now on my way to a deeper realization of the fellowship of the Spirit than I had ever experienced in my entire Christian walk...and that, coming from a pastor!

I was actually starting to sense God's presence like never before. However, what I noticed more was *the fruit* of this time of devotion. I was hearing God's voice with greater clarity throughout my activities and work. The frustration levels were dropping, and my perspective on everything was balancing out. I began to understand with greater depth the song, "Turn your eyes upon Jesus, look full in His wonderful face, and the things of earth will grow strangely dim; in the light of His glory and grace." Some of the things that had seemed important to me or that bothered me were now seemingly of no importance or significance. People around me were noticing something different; sometimes becoming overcome in the Spirit when I would walk up to them. Even Mary's and my personal devotion to, and enjoyment of one another, was being accentuated by the deeper fellowship of the Spirit... How could great get greater?

Once, at a prophetic conference we were attending, I received an interesting word. It stated that I should "spend time on the mountain." That I would "do OK if I didn't, but that I would prosper more if I would choose to do so." I knew what the word was referring to. It wasn't directing me to become a mountain man. But was in line with what God had already been saying about stealing time away with Him. As a result, I had decided to commit myself to two days a month away wherever I could find a place to accommodate the time. I tried various retreat centers in our area, until I finally found the one that would work best. As a busy pastor it has never been convenient to go away. My schedule is seldom "open" for this; yet I will make the choice to go and somehow everything else always manages to work out. It is in these times, that I can totally let my hair down (a metaphor, since I have little hair left these days)! It is there, I can seek, cry, speak out loud, move about (I often pace to help keep me focused), and be totally undistracted from the normal pressures of the ministry or life.

These times have been essential in keeping proper perspective, especially in the face of mounting dilemmas or frustrating circumstances. Both Mary and I are committed to these times away and will challenge each other when we see our attitudes slipping. "You need more time with the Father," Mary will tell me, when she sees I'm close to wanting to "strike the rock"... which is our special code for the spiritual analogy taken from the life of Moses when he got frustrated with those...those...people he was leading! (See Numbers 20:8-12) Sadly, Moses' frustration and subsequent angry outburst (misrepresentation of the Lord), cost him his inheritance! Sometimes we actually ask each other "Are you ready to strike the rock, and lose your inheritance?" How I do when I'm by myself and anonymous... such as how I respond when cut off by someone in the car, also gives me a clue as to my need to get away. The miracle is how "everyone" seems to change for the better when I get back. It reminds me of the famous quote from Mark Twain, "When I was fourteen, my father was so ignorant I could hardly stand to have him around. When I got to be twenty-one, I was astonished at how much he had learned in seven years." Something about spending time in God's presence changes the maturity level of our perspectives.

This change in perspective, that comes from being in the presence of the Lord, has over the years encouraged me, strengthened me, and opened up to me the greater realm of the supernatural as a lifestyle. Sowing in the Spirit has reaped a great harvest of increased dreams/revelation and word of knowledge. But, best of all, frustration is no longer my portion!

Chapter four

The Road Map
Tools to Live by

So, now you're probably saying, "Well, I could really use some tools. I don't think I have the discipline that is required to pray for such long periods of time...Help!" Well, in case you were wondering, more often than not, the keepers of the gates of hell are actually sitting, watching guard over our minds. The hellions of the enemy's domain are constantly waiting for opportunities to distract you from sweet communion with the Lord. They are well adept at throwing thought grenades your way! The toughest journey for our walk of intimacy actually lies in climbing our way up Jacob's ladder; from the muck and mire of earth's distractions (otherwise known as daily life), through the confusion and warfare of the devil's second heaven domain, straight into the throne room of our living God. So, what are some helpful tools that will help you persevere till you enter the Presence and can abide there?

Worship in Spirit and in Truth

Worship is a powerful key. The psalmist declares in Psalm 100:4, *"Enter into His gates with thanksgiving, and into His courts with praise; be thankful to Him and bless His Name."* The phrase "enter into His gates" has a much deeper meaning than we can discern at first glance. The word "enter" means to go to war or to invade. The root word for "gates" means to act as a gatekeeper. So, through the obedient act of thanksgiving, we will begin to open a portal into the presence of the Lord through invasion, warfare and acting as a gatekeeper over our minds. The only reference verse for the root word for "gates" is Proverbs 23:7, *"For as a man thinks in his heart, so is he..."* The word "thinks" is this same word "gates" or "to act as a gatekeeper." Here is an important truth... *Our thoughts ARE the gates, either to Heaven or to hell.* So...you could reword the proverb like this... "For as a man (acts like a wise gatekeeper over) his heart, so *IS* he..." If we truly believe that God is praiseworthy, then our actions will follow suit, and our contrary mindsets, will and emotions will be subdued. We will then become full of praise! The word of God tells us that praise is "becoming" for the "upright." It's an attractive garment that we should dress ourselves up in every day!

Four of the Hebrew words for praise are listed in this one verse: **Towdah, Tehillah, Yadah** and **Barak**:

Towdah means...to worship with extended hands, adoration, confession and choral singing

Tehillah means... to praise by making a show and being clamorously foolish

Yadah means... to revere or worship with extended hands, thanksgiving

Barak means... *to kneel down in praise*

There are many other words for worship that include acts of singing, dancing, twirling, writhing, lying prostrate and shouting. Once, many years ago, when I was first learning about praise and worship; I happened to be watching a documentary about Israel on public television. As the camera man zeroed in on a group of men praying by the Wailing Wall, the announcer, in a very dry, and heavy English accent made a profound statement. He said, "I suppose you are wondering why the Jews sway back and forth while they are saying their prayers...It is because they believe the commandment that they are to worship the Lord with their whole being." To a former Presbyterian, who had qualms about raising hands during a worship service, it all suddenly made sense! We were to worship the Lord with every part of our being and with all of our strength.

When we worship extravagantly, we subdue our flesh and our souls (mind, will and emotions). We also bring our tongue, which can sometimes be an unruly beast, under Christ's lordship! David didn't always feel like worshipping even though he was a worshipper at heart. Sometimes he just had bad days, like we all do. But, during those rough seasons of life, he would command his soul to rise up and bless the Lord. He would say, "Bless the Lord oh my soul, and ALL that is within me bless His Holy Name!" Not just some, not just part, but ALL. Worship is something that involves our whole being! We bring before the Lord all that we have and all that we are. That is why it is called the sacrifice of praise. When it comes with tears, it is all the more precious to the Lord. The Word of God tells us that He actually collects those tears in a bottle. Worship has nothing at all to do with our feelings; it is about Worth-ship. It's the acknowledgement of God's greatness and worthiness. He is worthy of all our praise and all our heart's affection.

The Power of Right Confession

A great place to start is by reading some of the

Psalms out loud and personalizing them. Why should we speak them out loud? Scripture gives us two really great motivations. One is, *"the Word is near you and even in your mouth,"* and *"faith comes by hearing, and hearing by the Word of God."* The truth of God's word (Jesus Himself) is so near to you, He's in you, even right in your mouth. Let Him out! There is power that is released through confession (notice that some of the words for worship have to do with loud confession and declaration). *"Death and life are in the power of the tongue..."* (Proverbs 18:21) The word "power" also means a hand (the open one) indicating power, means and direction. The tongue is truly a powerful weapon.

The second reason is that actually physically hearing declarations of faith coming out of our own mouths begins to activate real faith in our hearts. Paul actually admonished husbands to wash their wives with the "water of the Word." The Word has a built in purifying effect. Perhaps it's high time to start "brain" "washing" our minds with the Living Word! Start with this declaration from Psalm 118:24, *"This is the day that the Lord has made; (I) will rejoice and be glad in it!"* The word "made" in this verse means to have charge of. Do you believe that Jesus has charge of EVERY day in your lifetime...even the seemingly bad ones? If you declare it enough, you'll start to believe it. There were days that were so rough during our early days of ministry, days of disappointment and betrayal; that we would begin to come into the Lord's presence weeping as we made these confessions and proclamations from God's word. But, the truth is, no matter what we think we perceive with our human eyes, God is ONLY good and ONLY does good things. Sometimes buildings during the building process look a bit messy! Often we forget this as we look at the building process of our lives. God is building something in our lives that will house His glory. God doesn't do quick works. He does works that will last.

If anyone besides the Lord would have been watching me (Mary) trying to struggle through to the place of breakthrough in my prayer times during those early years, I'm certain they would have thought I was crazy! It was truly pitiful at times. Often, I would go into our church sanctuary and put the words to our ministry's theme song up on the overhead (I call it our theme song, because it was given to us by the Lord through a simultaneous supernatural visitation and dream that we both had one morning when He first commissioned us as a ministry). Then, I'd start singing through a veil of tears and with a sheer act of my will (because nothing in the natural seemed to be going right), *"My hope is built on nothing less than Jesus' blood and righteousness. I dare not trust the* sweetest frame, but wholly lean on Jesus name." This particular phrase was often met with an assault of memories of recent personal betrayals! Or, on the days that were filled with unanswered questions and seeming contradictions, I would choke out these words, *"When darkness hides his lovely face, I rest on His unchanging grace. When all around my soul gives way; my anchor holds within the veil. On Christ the solid rock I stand. All other ground is sinking sand. All other ground is sinking sand!"* This was worship in its purest and most raw form. What was amazing, was that as I continued to press through, eventually the discouragement would lift, and my heart would be flooded with supernatural peace. The enemy knows this to be true, so he is always battling us for who we will worship during times of trouble. If he can dissuade us, he can keep us from the One who has the solutions for our trials.

The God of Breakthrough

King David understood the secret of choosing to press through to the place of breakthrough, when all hell seems to be raging against you. As we mentioned earlier, the lessons of his youth surely prepared him for his future as ruler over Israel. His many hours spent with God out in the hillsides of Judea, taught him Who his Source of strength was, and how to not only hear... but to also cooperate with the Spirit.

Shortly after becoming king, David sought the Lord about going to war against the Philistines who were already gathered against him. The Lord sent him forth with Israel into battle and gave the enemy into their hands. After the enemy was thoroughly defeated, David declared, "...God has broken in upon my enemies by my own hand, like the breakthrough of many waters. Therefore he called the place, Baal-Perazim (Master of the Breakthrough)." Even though David knew he could do nothing without the Lord, he was aware that God often breaks through in situations through our cooperation and obedience. He uses our own hands in partnership and agreement with His purposes, to achieve breakthrough.

Sometimes putting on praise and worship music can help you to enter in and achieve the breakthrough that's needed. Just be sure to focus on the One who is the object of your affection, or you can easily be distracted by the music itself. Then, it can become all about the singing. It's also important, if you're going to use music to help you enter in, that you choose songs that truly glorify the Lord and make positive declarations about His character. Be careful not to pick songs that are self focused or that talk about your needs, wants or desires. Also, be careful to pick songs that are more about the character of the Lord than His attributes. The idea is to focus more on who He is, than what He does, unless you're in desperate need of convincing that He is good in your life. So, in that case, those songs can be a good beginning place of proclamation, which will help you work your way toward true worship of the King of Kings. In time you may want to shift to more non-descript wordless music that is worshipful...often called soaking music. This allows you to enter in without getting distracted by the words or the song itself.

Waging War with the Prophetic

Another great practice that will help you to begin to "stay your mind" on the Lord, is to declare your personal prophetic promises out loud. It is helpful to write them out, and keep a prophetic journal. You can do this with your significant dreams as well. Paul actually instructed Timothy to "wage war" with the prophecies that had been spoken over him. (See I Timothy 1:18) By declaring these promises out loud, you are, as scripture encourages, speaking to the things that are not as though they already existed. This activates your faith to believe the Lord for the fulfillment of these promises that He's given to you. You can actually take your prophetic journal and declare key promises directly from it...thanking the Lord that His promises are "yes and amen" and that He is "faithful to bring to completion" the good work that He has begun in your life. It again is a good idea to speak these promises out loud, as faith is activated by hearing.

The "Stayed" Mind

Isaiah 26:3 says, *"You will keep him in perfect peace, whose mind is stayed on You, because he trusts You."* All of these methods are really just meant to achieve this one goal...and that is to bring your soul to a place of rest and peace. The pathway to this is learning how to "stay your mind" on the Lord, as we mentioned earlier. The word "stayed" simply means **to rest self, to lie hard, to lean upon, or to take hold of.** In a strange way, as we are leaning on the Lord, we are allowing Him to put our disquieted soul to sleep. We will begin to manifest His supernatural peace as we lean on Him. The Lord desires to "quiet us in His love." He desires to silence the storm that is in our mind so that we can hear Him. Have you ever noticed how often the Lord will speak to us in the still and quiet hours of the morning, before all the hustle and bustle of the day begins? This is the same type of peaceful surrender the Lord desires us to accomplish during our times alone with Him. He would love to be able to speak to us 24-7, but we must first learn how to quiet our souls.

Meditation is not a Bad Word

Another very affective method for bringing our souls into a place of rest is learning how to meditate on God's word. Sometimes it can be helpful to meditate on a favorite passage of Scripture. On many occasions during your prayer times, the Lord may choose to highlight a verse that He is trying to speak to you through. One day I was sitting by the river praying, and the Lord caused a verse to become illuminated in my heart. I began to repeat it aloud over and over as it was going through my mind… "Light is sown like seed for the righteous." The Lord, at that time, was beginning to speak to me about His light of revelation, and this was His way of getting my attention. Another time, the Lord highlighted three different phrases… "Unless a seed fall to the ground"… "Poured out like a drink offering"…and "Deep speaks to deep." Little did I know at the time, that the Lord was going to let our seed fall to the ground, and that He was going to pour us out till there was nothing left, and that when we fell into the deep dark hole…that then He would speak to us in the "deep" places! Sometimes it is His encouragement that warns us of trouble that's on the way. The word "meditate" in scripture actually means **to revolve in the mind**. Picture yourself caught in a revolving door! You're actually trying to create a loop in your mind that excludes wayward thoughts.

That's why it's important to know and to memorize scripture (not during your times of seeking, but in preparation during your study times). If you find scripture memorization difficult, try putting a meaningful verse to music. Pick an easy favorite tune... something memorable like a Christmas melody, and then insert the words of the verse you love. Sing it with all your heart, till it becomes part of you. Or, try writing the verse on several 3x5 cards. Place the cards in strategic places that you'll see throughout the day, like your bathroom mirror, your car's dashboard or the refrigerator. Say the verse out loud every time you see it. You'll soon find God's word penetrating your thought life. Jesus used the scripture to combat the devil's lies and accusations... why shouldn't we? Remember, that God's word is "living and active." It's sharper than a "two-edged sword," and it's able to penetrate and divide between "bone and marrow." That's pretty sharp and extremely precise! Don't you think it can also cut away the thoughts that aren't God's from your mind? Practice this every day, and soon God's thoughts will become your thoughts!

A Quiet Place, Alone

As you prepare for your time alone with God, make sure you pick a quiet place with little or no distraction. Earplugs or sound canceling head phones can help if quiet places are not readily available. Some people I know actually clear out a small spot in their closets, if they have small homes! If distraction is a possibility, the enemy will be sure to use it. Turn off your cell phones. Only a short number of years ago, none of us even had them, and somehow we managed to survive! Make sure you have tissue nearby, and water is helpful too. It's important to have your Bible handy, so the Lord can speak to you out of His word. Just be careful not to go into study mode (especially all you teacher types!)

As a matter of fact, when you finally begin to break through you might begin to get all kinds of great insights and scriptural ideas for teaching and sermons; however, you must keep in mind that this is not the goal of your time with the Lord. Just jot down a short reminder so you can come back to it later, when you're actually prepared to study. Your goal is to press into a place of communion with the Lord that goes beyond surface revelations. So, as you can see, it's a good idea to have something handy to write with, since it is easy to forget spiritual insights, but make them brief and then move forward. Spiritual insights can be quite fleeting and if we don't act on them by writing them down, they will dissipate like an early morning dream. Just don't get stuck there. Even a recording device can be beneficial for recording your visions and words. I actually enjoy having a pillow and blanket handy, because once I have entered into the Presence; I generally like to be very still.

When we are taking time alone with the Lord,

sometimes we like to pace or to walk as we begin to pray. I usually start with proclaiming the names of God, and personalizing them by thanking the Lord for manifesting His attributes and benefits in our lives every day. I declare His goodness according to each part of His nature, which is bound up in the understanding of the various names of God. There are many names for God that are identified in scripture, and they make a wonderful study. As I pray, I tie these names for God with specific scriptures that refer to the character of each name... thanking Him for His attributes that are manifesting in my life. For example I might pray, "I praise you Jehovah Shalom for You are the God of peace, and I thank You that the peace that passes all understanding will rule in our hearts and minds today...and that you will keep us in perfect peace as we willingly stay our minds on You... and because You are the God of peace, You will soon crush satan under our feet...and I praise You Lord for causing us to become as those who have found peace in Your eyes...and that there shall be no end to the increase of Your government or of your peace!" This is just one example of how you can praise the name of the Lord. Notice that these are all phrases straight from scripture. In my ongoing prayer life, I try to run every day into the name of the Lord, for it is a "high tower" that the righteous can "run into and be safe!"

Then, often, I will spend time binding us to

Kingdom reality, that the Kingdom of God will be present in our lives here on earth as it already is in Heaven. "Let Your Kingdom come and Your will be done here on earth as it is in Heaven." For scripture tells us that whatever we "bind on earth" shall be what is already "bound in heaven." I will then go through the various areas of our lives and the lives of our children and grandchildren and bind us to the Lord's will in each of these physical and spiritual arenas. I begin to declare the things that are not yet seen in our lives, as though they already exist, because in Heaven they already do! But, it's important to remember that these suggestions, that are meant to help you focus, are what we refer to as gateway experiences. You're not meant to dwell at the gates... your goal is to enter in.

When the disciples asked the Lord how to pray, He actually gave them an outline for prayer called the "Lord's Prayer." We tend to pray it as is, without realizing that it is simply an outline to help us focus our minds. If you take each phrase from the Lord's Prayer and spend time praying each part, adding your own personal needs to it, then it should take you about an hour to pray. Here are a couple of examples from the Lord's Prayer that will help to focus your heart on Christ and His goodness in your life. When you come to the first part "Holy is Your name," concentrate on worshipping, using the various names of the Lord, as I suggested above. When you come to the section of the prayer "give us this day our daily bread (needs)," instead of asking for your needs to be met, try thanking the Lord for ALREADY supplying your needs abundantly one by one...for He already has provided for you "everything pertaining to life and Godliness." You'll be amazed at how thanking Him for already providing for you can release faith, joy and expectancy in your heart. Be careful not to get stuck in the place of need orientation, but instead let gratefulness arise from your heart. Remember the goal is to help prepare you for your intimate time with Him, and different methods that help to enter in will vary per individual. These are all just forms and patterns to get you started and focused. The real goal of course is to commune with the Lord.

Chapter five

Spirit Language
More than Y'all

One extremely important "tool" that is absolutely invaluable in helping you to commune with the Lord is the ability to "pray in the Spirit at all times"... also known as, praying in tongues. We can't help but notice these days, that many Spirit filled Christians, have stopped emphasizing the importance of this gift of tongues in the prayer life of every believer. Yes, it's true that not every believer has this gift...yet, it is clear in scripture, that every believer has EVERY gift at their disposal...and this particular one is so beneficial. Paul actually boasted in the Lord when he said, *"I thank my God I speak with tongues more than you all."* (See I Corinthians 14:18) It is the Lord's desire to fill you with His Spirit and to provide you complete access to the miraculous realm through the gifts of His Spirit.

The "Promise of the Father" known as the Baptism in the Holy Spirit, is for EVERYONE. (See Acts 2:39) As you ask Jesus to baptize you and fill you with His Spirit, you will be offered the "gifts of the Spirit." We are instructed to "earnestly desire" these gifts, which indicates that they are open and available to every believer. One very essential gift to ask the Lord for is the gift of tongues, because it becomes our spiritual prayer language.

It is important not to "grieve" the Holy Spirit by refusing any of these beautiful gifts that He freely showers us with. In many ways, He is like the friend of the bridegroom (best man) and therefore the representative for our beloved Jesus to whom we are betrothed. According to Jewish culture, after the betrothal, the groom would actually withdraw until the wedding day, and the groomsman would be the sole representative of the groom's wishes to the bride. He would bring all communication and special gifts to the bride during the duration of the engagement. The bride would never dream of sending the gifts back. This bridal picture is a perfect analogy of our relationship to the Holy Spirit. To refuse the gifts that Jesus has sent to us through His personal representative, the Holy Spirit, is to in effect... refuse Him. EVERY gift given is of great value, because they are tokens of His affection toward us. We must understand His heart and value what He values.

The benefits of praying in tongues are numerous, but one crucial element is the ability to pray long. As you pray in the Holy Spirit, there is a peaceful abiding that begins to settle on you. It occurs as your spirit man enters into cooperation with the Holy Spirit's agenda. As your own desires and needs come into subjection to the Holy Spirit's perfect prayer, you in effect give complete direction over to the Spirit's desires. He becomes the "pilot" and you become the "co-pilot." Romans 8:26-27 accurately describes the process, *"Likewise the Spirit also helps in our weaknesses. For we do not know what we should pray for as we ought, but the Spirit Himself makes intercession for us with groanings which cannot be uttered. Now He who searches the hearts knows what the mind of the spirit is, because He makes intercession for the saints according to the will of God."*

We have literally spent days away communing in the presence of the Lord, and one thing that has helped us to do so, is the ability to pray in the Spirit. We are instructed in scripture to "pray without ceasing." One way this instruction is even possible is by praying in tongues. Much like a babbling brook, praying in the Spirit will cause "rivers of living water" to "flow" out of our bellies. (See John 7:38-39) We should pray in the Spirit constantly all throughout the day, as we go about our business... sort of like keeping our engines continually running. This can be easily done as we do our daily activities, praying softly... just under our breath. It's good discipline, and will prepare you for long encounters with the Spirit when you have time alone with Him.

There are numerous benefits to speaking in tongues. One is that it builds you up in your faith. Jude 1:20 says, *"But you beloved, building yourselves up on your most holy faith, praying in the Holy Spirit."* Isaiah refers to this "stammering lips" and "another tongue" saying, "This is the rest with which You may cause the weary to rest." And, "This is the refreshing." (See Isaiah 28:11-12) The word "rest" in the above verses means **consolation (as in matrimony)**. We are to be married to the Lord, and in this, we truly find rest and consolation. It is His very nature to console us. So, we see listed in the above verses three very important reasons for exercising this gift...to be built up in our faith...to rest when we are weary...and to become refreshed.

There have even been scientific studies done that show that there is a specific part of the brain that apparently is only activated, when the subjects studied, were speaking in tongues. Also, at the University of Pennsylvania, Dr. Andrew Newberg did studies on the brain activity of individuals who speak in tongues. Newberg used CT scans to discover what occurs in the brains control center while speaking in tongues. Apparently, the frontal lobe, which is the part of the brain right behind the forehead, and is considered the brain's control center, goes "quiet" as those studied began to pray in tongues. Newberg said, "When they are actually engaged in this whole very intense spiritual practice... their frontal lobes tend to go down in activity...that's in fairly stark contrast to the Buddhist and Franciscan nuns- in prayer...in those individuals the frontal lobes actually increase activity." (2007 ABC News Internet Ventures) What occurs in our physical bodies as we begin to pray in the Spirit, is obviously a mysterious design from the Lord. It appears that the activation of our spirit man causes our souls (our mind...control center) to become subdued and quieted...as part of our brain actually rests while a specialized zone of the brain is activated.

The word says, *"For the promise (the gift of the Holy Spirit) is for you... and for... as many as the Lord our God shall call to Himself."* (Acts 2:39 NAS) Are you one that the Lord has called to Himself? Why don't you pause with us right now and ask Jesus to baptize you with His Holy Spirit? He will fill you again and again as you ask Him to. If this is your first time to do so, expect Him to come bringing gifts with Him... and don't forget to open them!

Lord, I ask you to baptize me this day with Your

Holy Spirit. You are good, and you said in your word that if I ask you for bread that You won't give me a stone... and how much more You would give me more of the Holy Spirit if I ask You. So, today Lord, I'm coming to You as a child and I'm asking. Send me the Spirit without measure... Your joy that is unspeakable and full of glory! Fill me Lord! Holy Spirit I welcome You. Come Lord! In Jesus' precious Name... AMEN.

Now, wait and see what He will do!

Chapter Six

Seeing His Face
The Kisses of the Son

At the opening of Song of Solomon, the Shulamite makes a bold declaration. She says, *"Let him kiss me with the kisses of his mouth- For your love is better than wine. Because of the fragrance of your good ointments, Your name is ointment poured forth; Therefore the virgins love you. Draw me away!"* (Song of Solomon 1:1-4a) One of the meanings for "kiss" is to **equip with weapons**. As we are touched by, or fastened to the Lord, we become equipped to encounter our daily lives. More importantly, we become strengthened to face the battle and stand up against the accusations that the enemy often throws our way. One of the most perfect prayers mentioned in the Word of God is only three words, and it lies at the beginning of verse 4... *"Draw me away!"* The word "draw" means **to sow**. Again, it is the idea of intimacy... the sowing of seed. All conception requires an act of intimacy. There is a sowing in the Spirit that occurs as we spend time with Jesus in face to face encounters. The Biblical principle of "reaping what you sow" was never truer than in our time spent with God.

Why is it, that we Christians often seek to birth things that have not, yet, been conceived through the spiritual act of intimacy? We often labor and struggle to push out something that hasn't, yet, been created, or fully developed in the secret place. There is a spiritual conception that occurs as we allow ourselves to come under the shadow of the Most High. It requires alone time with God. After her initial plea for the Lord to "draw" her, the Shulamite makes another request. In Song of Solomon 4:16 she calls out to the north and south winds, *"Awake...Blow upon* **my garden,** *that its spices may flow out."* Then she makes a dramatic shift in her understanding. She says, "Let my beloved come into **His garden**..." At this point, in her relationship with the King, she has a personal awakening, and suddenly realizes that she is utterly, totally His, and His alone. The Lord is moved by our passion for Him. It is a choice we alone can choose to make...to beg Him to "draw us"...and to beg Him for an even deeper touch...an awakening. If we will make this choice, then our garden will become His garden. Our fellowship with the Son will deepen and mature.

The ultimate goal, of course, is that we would have this same spiritual awakening that the Shulamite experienced. We are instructed throughout the book of Song of Solomon, not to, "stir up nor awaken love until it pleases." This is a cooperative effort. If we desire a spiritual awakening, we must press for it. Like the Shulamite, we must pursue this awakening. We must move beyond the point of hesitation, and be willing to respond quickly to our Beloved's overtures. When He calls, we must not hesitate to come. This is part of the maturation of the Bride of Christ. We were created for His pleasure. We were made for Him. There is no greater pleasure on Earth than to be wholly His. One of God's ultimate desires is for you to learn how to be *"joyful in (His) house of prayer."* (See Isaiah 56:7)

Once during a season of desperate pursuit for greater intimacy with the Lord, I had a God encounter that radically changed my world. I was trying to push aside the demands of others on my life, having just finished a very long fast. I happened to be attending a conference with some other people, and had opted out of one of the sessions, in response to the beckoning of the Spirit. It was obvious that the folks I was with were not pleased over my decision, but I was trying to allow the "fear of the Lord" to reign over my heart more than the "fear of man."

So, it was as I sat by the river not far from the conference we had been enjoying, trying not to worry about having offended the people I was supposed to be with, that I poured out my longings to the Lord. I asked Him, "Why is it that sometimes I'm hot for you, and sometimes I'm not?" I was speaking from a heart that was discouraged by all the things in my life that tended to drain passion for the Lord right out of me... people with constant expectations for one! Then, the Lord responded with that familiar sweet and undeniable clarity within my spirit, "My daughter, it's because you are stuck in Song of Solomon 5:3." I opened to the passage (one I didn't immediately recognize) and read, *"I have taken off my dress. How can I put it on again? I have washed my feet. How can I dirty them again?"* The passage begins with the woman's beloved knocking at the door, desiring to be with her. The woman hesitates because the hour is late, and she is already asleep... cozy and warm in her bed. As I read the words in front of me, I heard the Lord say, "I am about to move you past the point of hesitation." In my heart, I begged Him to do it. From that day forward, I found myself growing in my availability to the tug of the Spirit on my heart... even if it meant pulling away from the needs of the crowd.

The distractions in our lives, known as the "tyranny

of the urgent," cause us to hesitate when the Lord calls us. His desire is that we would become the "prepared bride," the one who has "made herself ready." No one can make you prepare your heart to meet with the Lord. No one can force you to respond to His call when it comes at an inconvenient moment. This is something only you can do for yourself. It comes through a searching and available heart. It comes as we ask him to "awaken love" within us.

Chapter seven

Facing Distractions
If at first you don't succeed

The real trick in this intimate seeking, is establishing a consistent time of seeking. Mary laughs at me when I finally make a decision to do something. Often, (take exercise, for example) I'll approach a new discipline like this...I will make charts, weigh myself, measure my waist, buy new tennis shoes and then hit the gym with full gusto! Not to mention the pictures I have her snap for what I like to call my "BEFORE PORTFOLIO." I'll feel great after my day's endeavors and so accomplished. Then comes the next day....I can't move, let alone continue my new found discipline. And so, it was a valiant attempt, but the memory of the pain now works against my new resolve. And, before I know it, I've petered out of my new discipline.

This illustration is also what I've done, and heard many do as well, when it comes to spending time with God. The heart is right, the desire is there, but if we are not careful, we will bite off more than we can chew and sabotage our own efforts to succeed. Internally, we want to be seekers, and now that we've decided to really put feet to the task, just putting in 15 minutes or a half hour doesn't seem sufficient. Yet, if you are not use to spending communing time with the Lord, then 15 minutes might be just right in the beginning, especially if you will consistently do 15 minutes a day. Like exercise, it is about disciplining ourselves in focus and resting, so that we begin to press into the deeper place in God. They say that if you stop exercising your physical body for more than two days, that the progress you've made to date begins to immediately diminish; and when you begin again, you actually have to retake ground that you once possessed. This is what it is like to develop the discipline of pure seeking time in the Lord. If you only do it sporadically, you in effect lose ground and it is like starting over each time. Drawing into God's presence is progressive and cumulative. So it is better to start small, and increase incrementally, than to try to start big and only hit and miss in your times with the Lord. Don't wait for it to just work out. The enemy will make sure it doesn't. You will need to actively schedule time with God, and keep your new discipline with resolve.

The Distractions of the enemy

The last thing the devil wants is to see you commune with God, and one of his strongest tactics, is to distract us from our goal. That is why it is so important to find a place that leaves little, or no, distraction potentials. Shut off cell phones, get away from people who can't leave you alone, don't multi-task. Studies have shown that we don't truly multi-task effectively anyway; we just diminish productivity in each task attempted. So trying to commune, truly commune with God, in the car while driving for example, is not a place to successfully stay focused because of the necessity for safe driving. It can be part of your God walk; but not the type of communing that we've been talking about. In addition, try to find a place that won't activate your need to become task oriented. A work place, or office, may pull you toward activity and not rest, even though you weren't really planning on doing those tasks anyway.

As I mentioned earlier, when we first started this quest, I could not find a place to pray that was distraction free, so I would drive out into the boonies and try to find a place to park and just commune with God. I want to revisit my testimony with you again because of its vivid spiritual implications. As I would find some turn-off, shut off the engine and roll down my window; I would begin to praise God and pull on

His presence. Within 5 minutes of my soaking time, remember how inevitably a car would come by and pull over and actually park next to me? It didn't matter that I was in the middle of nowhere! So...end of private time. Weird! But, can you recognize the other-world influence that repeatedly tried to stop me? And, you must also realize...it will try to stop you, too.

Seeking is a serious endeavor. Do you really think the enemy is going to curtsy and let us easily have our communing time with the Lord, when he knows the power that exists in its fruit? We must be aware that the devil will resist every attempt we make to draw closer to the heart of God. It is a spiritual battle, one that threatens the enemy...we must begin to press from our earthbound-ness, past the second heavens where the devil is flying around with his giant cymbals and brass band, and as we continue to press, eventually, we will gloriously be welcomed into the third heavens where the throne room of Christ awaits our bold entry! Don't even be surprised, if in your pursuit of the Lord's presence (even in the deeper places), that the enemy comes with the most perverse thoughts and impressions to distract you. Remember, the devil showed up in the middle of Jesus' forty day fast, despite the presence of an open heaven where the angels of God were tending to Him! The devil plays dirty. He doesn't play by the rules, and he definitely hits below the belt.

So why bother, some might ask? Well, the truth is, while resistance is there... it is not futile! The Spirit of God is drawing us if we will heed His invite, and with a little persistence, we can truly dwell or tabernacle with the love of our life.

That Stinkin' Flesh

It would be really nice if we could blame EVERYTHING on the devil. But, we do still have our flesh to deal with; which, in addition, scripture says also works against the things of the Spirit. Once distraction is dealt with from a practical dimension, there is still the pull of the flesh, at least in the beginning, that wants to back out of the deal. Your spirit is willing and you have decided to press into this quest of greater communion; yet, a part of you is ready to do other things. Uncompleted tasks, all of sudden, can come to mind: cleaning the garage, dishes, or house, returning those phone calls, cleaning the gutter....things you weren't planning on doing...ever, all of a sudden seem urgent.

In many ways, pressing into communion with the Lord (on a consistent basis) is a killing of the flesh; a death process. You will battle through to victory sometimes with real focus, and at other times, battle against sheer boredom. You will have times, when despite your good intention, God just seems far away and you feel ever so aware that you are just sitting in a room with four walls and a ceiling. But, take these times in stride; know that there will be some hits and misses, some dry times, some boring times, as well as some battle times; and that this is just part of the process of disciplining yourself toward a goal that is well worth the effort. There will also be some thrilling and fulfilling times. It is much like a building when it is first being built. Scaffolding is erected, at first, to give support. But the scaffolding is never meant to remain there; eventually the building will stand on its own.

And, so it is in this process...you may have to do some gyrations at first to keep your focus, but eventually the new discipline will stand on its own and so will the thrill of this deeper experiential relationship with God. Remember, God wants this time with you more than you do. Don't allow yourself to get frustrated. We have seen even ministers' eyes well up with tears when we mention pressing into the Lord....because they have tried this so many times and gotten frustrated and given up. Give yourself the room for some inconsistency. Schedules change, life's pressures change; but press with persistence toward a goal of constant seeking. As you continue to woo the Spirit, He will see that you really mean it and that you really want time with Him, and He will begin to make Himself known. Despite the resistance that was facing

Jesus and the ultimate fate awaiting Him, scripture says He "set His face" to go to Jerusalem. He was resolute. We too, can set our face to press into God's presence and find the joy of sitting at His feet. We often say it...God's favorite game is Hide and Seek. God loves to hide Himself *for us*, not from us.

Some time ago, I was at our favorite retreat place to spend time with the Lord. I had wanted to go on a nearby bluff that overlooked the valley where this retreat center was built. I had heard from others how awesome it could be worshipping God on this outcropping of rock. So, seeing that the retreat center was pretty empty of people, I started the hike and wound my way up the hill to the "rock." What people had told me was true....it was beautiful and awe inspiring! I found a spot on the very edge, foot dangling over the precipice, and began to pray. I was utterly alone, high above all surroundings, and the overall sense of God's presence was beginning to descend upon me.

Then panic hit me. I saw a runner coming up the path, stopping and looking at me every few feet. I thought, "Oh, no you don't. You're not going to ruin my time with God. I rebuke that runner from coming up here, in Jesus name!" I don't know if you are suppose to pray that way since he was probably a fine Christian on his own spiritual quest, but I was determined to not lose the moment. To my delight I watched as the runner suddenly stopped, turned around and started to jog back to the Center. "Yea, Lord! Thank You!" I cried out, and began to settle back down to worship.

However, my joy was short lived, as within about 10 minutes, I now saw a group of young adults coming up the trail. I cried out to the Lord again, but this time to no avail. It wasn't long, and the young adults were within ear shot of my prayers and so I settled into a posture and body language that I thought would clearly indicate that I was deep in prayer. I probably looked a bit like the Hunchback of Notre Dame, perched on my tower! One of the young men approached me and wanted to chat, but I was courteously brief and he got the hint and went a stone's throw away and began to pray as well. I wish his comrades had followed suit; but to my chagrin; one of the girls pulled out her cell phone and began to talk with her dad within feet of where I sat. I thought, "Does she not see I'm praying?" I contemplated turning and saying something, but the place was public property and they had just as much right to be there as I did. Then I mused to myself, "How long can a phone call be, I'll just wait it out." I sat there as she finished talking to her dad in a voice similar to Alvin and the Chipmunks on helium....and then it was, "Hello, Mom!".....then after that it was, "Hello, Grams!"....and then came her uncle and a plethora of cousins...to my utter disbelief, it seemed like she went through the whole family lineage! I thought, "Come on now!"

But, I had a choice to make...I certainly knew from experience that finding another lonesome spot was simply not going to happen. The question I was forced to ask myself, hit me... "Was I going to let this disrupt any further, what I was here for; or was I going to press into God's presence?" Thankfully, I made the correct choice. I subtly plugged my ears and began to pray silently in the Spirit. I was going to be resolute. Over a half hour went by, but eventually the young people disappeared one by one, ending with the girl on the phone. I was now alone...and I remained alone for the next two hours as I enjoyed an incredible time of communion with the Lord. To think, I had almost thrown the whole thing away....but persistence pays off. And, it will for you as well. Don't lose heart in doing well (in this case, pursuing His heart).

Chapter eight

The Glory Zone
Entering the Zone

Having said what we stated in the last chapter let me assure you, there will indeed be times of real breakthrough...times where it feels like you are literally just basking in His glory. At a certain point in your prayer time, you will actually discover this place of breakthrough that we're talking about. It's almost as though the very atmosphere around you begins to change. You are finally in "the zone." Right before this moment, (and this is a VERY important truth to realize) can actually be a time of great distraction. It can feel like you're facing an impenetrable wall, but trust me when I tell you...it's an illusion. The wall is actually a very thin veil that separates you from the eternal realm. Many, many people give up at this point. All we can say to you is, "Don't give up!" Make sure to press through that uncomfortable and dis-tracted place. DO NOT STOP!

If you continue to enter in, the result can be very serene times...periods of great peace or moments of great joy. You can be overcome with tears or laughter. This is the place of His touch. After pressing through the invisible veil, you will then begin to enjoy a great and profound sense of His pleasure. THIS IS YOUR GOAL AND DESTINATION...IT'S HIM! And, you'll dis-cover, that even time itself, will seem to stand still. You may lose awareness of your physical surround-ings. Remember that this is NOT the time to present your lists or suggestions to the Lord. That's the mis-take that Peter made when he was on the Mountain of Transfiguration with Jesus. The heavens had opened up; Peter was overwhelmed by what he saw, so he suggested that he could make some taberna-cles for Moses, Elijah and the now radiant Jesus, who were appearing before him. That was the end of the vision, and Peter found himself flat on the ground! Jesus had taken them up to the mountain to spend time with His Father. Peter got distracted by all the trappings, and forgot the real reason they were there. At that time, the Father said to them regarding His be-loved Son, "Hear Him." That day, as Jesus touched Peter and his two friends while they lay there on the ground, their eyes were finally open to see "Jesus only." That's the only way we will truly "hear Him" fully...as we behold Him. It's always been about spending time with Him and listening. It was then...It is now. (See Matthew 17:1-8)

When we've chosen to come away with the Lord, it should be a time to just enjoy Him for who He is. It is a lot like when a couple is going away on a honeymoon. It's not really about the place or the activities (for that just helps to create the proper atmosphere), but it's about the object of your affection. It's about receiving love...and giving love...to the One you love.

The REAL Breakthrough

Sometimes when we first get started and we've managed to push away distractions, we're worshipping and delighting ourselves in God...we suddenly reach a place, this special place of breakthrough, where we finally begin to get all these great insights. I've mentioned it before...this is NOT actually the "place" you are looking for. It's truly not the ultimate destination. The place you want is actually further in. Often times, particularly for preachers or teachers, it is very tempting to stop here, thinking you've arrived, and take notes....but press further in. Likewise, you may encounter at the onset a real revelation of your sinfulness, as the spirit of repentance falls on you....press even further. Almost immediately, the Lord will display His grace and mercy; with an overwhelming sense of His love....but DON'T EVEN STOP

THERE. These are all entrance experiences; this is still just the beginning....hunger for more and press deeper in.

As His presence overtakes you, you may actually feel His physical presence, or sometimes even feel, or hear the sound of wind. Some people have even heard footsteps, or heard the Lord calling to them. It is also possible to enter into visions, trances and spiritual experiences at this time. You may also hear the still, small voice of the Lord speaking to you within your heart. However, please don't get discouraged if this is not your exact experience. We are all unique. If you watch an earthly father play with his children, you will notice that each one of his kids reacts differently. They are all enjoying daddy's attention, but they each respond in their own special way. Your main goal is to abide in His vine, and let His fruit manifest in your life. There have been countless times that we have waited before the Lord and in the physical, sensed little if anything... yet the evidence of His presence and fruit in our lives after the fact was powerful. In fact, the actual prayer time may have felt more like an enormous waste of time than encountering the living God! Your gauge, and the ultimate question you are free to measure your experience by, is simply this... "Is the Kingdom of God manifesting in my life in greater measure?" The word tells us that His Kingdom is "righteousness, peace and joy in the Holy Spirit."

Once, as we were spending time together seeking the Lord in the sanctuary of the store-front church during our early years as a ministry, the Lord spoke a word clearly to our hearts in perfect unison...a strange experience to be sure! It was quiet, yet precise, in clarity. Had we not been so completely relaxed, and postured to hear, we would have missed it utterly. It seemed at first that we were having one of those uneventful sessions in His presence...since we had been waiting on the Lord for quite some time, with no outward manifestations of the Spirit at all. We were actually lying on the floor on opposite sides of the sanctuary, almost asleep, just basking quietly in Jesus. It was simply one of those very quiet, non-remarkable, yet peaceful times.

Suddenly, the Spirit interrupted the silence with a supernatural download. We each received the identical word of knowledge at the same precise moment. The word had to do with a relational issue of offence, regarding a couple who were members of our church at the time. We sat up abruptly...looked startled at each other...shared with each other what we had heard, and promptly stood up, locked up the building, jumped in the car and headed toward the couple's house. En-route, we received another download from the Spirit. "Did you hear that?" I asked. "Yes, I did," replied Kim. It was more information regarding another couple that apparently, according to the Holy

Spirit's direction, we were going to also find waiting for us at the first couple's house. It is really important for you to understand, that in the natural, we had NO inkling that trouble was brewing. This news flash from the Lord was truly news to us! Had it not been for the Spirit's counsel, we would have been taken by complete surprise...as the relational conflict would have literally blown up in our faces. Because of the Holy Spirit's warning, we were able to handle the situation in a peaceable and wise manner... under the banner of His love. So, you see, you must never underestimate even the very subtle and seemingly uneventful times of soaking in the Lord's presence!

In time, as you continue to go deeper and deeper, you will also discover doorways into heavenly places where untold riches of the Spirit await you. Many of these doorways will become familiar to you and easier and easier to access, but be sure to maintain your sense of awe...a sort of holy discontentment, that causes you to stay on this journey. You will find "joy, unspeakable and full of glory" as you press into the face of God. Dreams and visions will come to you, not as you seek the gifts, but as you seek the Giver! As you make Him your goal and destination...whether subtle or powerful...you'll never be disappointed.

Chapter nine

Intimate Encounter
Sowing and Reaping

It's different for everyone, but sometimes we expect that pressing into the Lord's presence will automatically bring us into some marvelous time of glory. That's what makes the journey of discovery, both varied and continually interesting. We may expect goose bumps, the sound of angels singing, or a manifestation or experience that we heard someone else has encountered. Mary sometimes hears doves cooing or bells ringing...a manifestation that some, but NOT ALL who have been in the room with her at the time have heard as well. I have felt angels brush by me at times. However, I also remember sitting there as I was first learning to practice His presence, almost like I was trying to open up my head to receive all that God had. I was opening up the hatch, like some large cargo ship, and saying to God, "Here I am, fill me up!" The Lord deals with us individually; and while there can be some glorious moments; at lot of the time is just plain waiting on the Lord and loving on Him.

Despite our feeling that He may already know it, the Lord loves to hear us tell Him how much we love Him. He loves to be adored. The main thing to keep in mind, is, that this time we have set aside is for Him (not only for us) and that we have purposed to give Him this time exclusively, because we love Him. But, whether or not you have immediate dynamic encounters, the effort is not wasted. If we sow in the Spirit (and spending time with God is definitely that) then we will also reap in the Spirit. You will begin to see the effects of your times with God in the daily on-goings of life. His voice will become clearer. You really will begin to experience dreams and visions, etc. Don't become impatient, but just enjoy the view along the way. Remember, it is the overflow of His Spirit that begins to produce an ever expanding reality in our lives. You are developing a lifestyle, not just an experience.

Romancing the Heart of God

For many years, off and on, we have led worship in our church services. Part of the art of entering into God's presence is starting with the awe inspiring greatness of God and moving toward the intimate.

We start with praise and proclamation, declaring the wonders of God's power and love for mankind. We marvel at His faithfulness to an undeserving people. We herald His steadfast kindness and atoning love for His creation. We proclaim His mighty victory over the enemy. We speak of the great things He has done. In essence, we often follow a format similar to the tabernacle in the wilderness or the temple that was in Jerusalem. We start in the outer court with thanksgiving and praise and proceed through the inner court or Holy place with our goal of entering reverently and worshipfully into the Holy of Holies. As we do, our love language begins to change. We go from generalities to specifics, from acts to ways, from broad to personal. Our communion with the Lord takes on a more sensitive and romantic posture to one of adoration and intimate worship.

But over the years we've notice that many of God's children get stuck in the outer court....they go on and on about His majestic-ness and His awesomeness; describing His appearance, His power and the outer workings of His hand. These are important facets to be thankful for, without a doubt; however, not where we want to remain. Imagine you are romancing the one you love and telling them how much you love the way they cook, clean the house, do the yard, play an instrument, take care of themselves, nurture the children, pay the bills, work and provide for the household, etc. Flattering, for sure, and it definitely shows an appreciation for what they do. But now imagine cuddling up together and looking into their eyes and still going on about how well they painted the living room. For most, this would be a mood killer. Or, worse yet, as you gaze lovingly into their eyes, you begin to tell them all that is troubling you. If this sounds familiar, you may need some marriage counseling! No one would view this as an intimate gesture.

Instead, they would want to know how you feel about *them*... not just about what they do. Yes, you might be sharing your heart of concerns, but they want to hear your emotions for them. They would want to know about your feelings and how you can't live without them; how you can hardly even breathe when they are gone, how you feel like only half a person without them, and desire nothing but to linger in their arms, feeling their heart beat and the warmth of their presence until the break of day. God loves this kind of language too. He created it. If you don't believe me, read the Song of Solomon: an analogy of the love relationship between the Lord and His people. As I've stated before... He loves to hear how much we adore Him; not because He is egotistical, but because He is the lover of our soul.

It's important that we don't get stuck in the grandiose, and potentially impersonal, exaltation of our beloved; but that we develop an intimate love language toward our All in All. If you are not verbose or articulate in this area, then pray in tongues or personalize some of the more intimate passages in Psalms, in between short, intimate phrases of your own of love, gratitude and appreciation. Remember, the Lord does not tire of hearing how much we love Him. There is a wooing that goes on in our relationship with the Lord. How intimate it was that John laid his head on the breast of Jesus; and how strongly Jesus desires that type of intimate communion with us as well.

We unfortunately live in an age where we want microwave results for our efforts. However, God is faithful, and He will reward those who diligently seek Him. I believe the truest reward actually is more of Him. So, whether you regularly enter into a tangible, discernable, glory zone... or just become enveloped in His "peace that" by "passes all" your frustrated "understanding," we guarantee you'll be hooked for life! And, we're certain that you'll definitely become transformed along the way. We hope that you delight in your new found joy as you seek more of the Lord's presence. And, that you find all the treasures He has hidden for you in the secret place! Remember, He is your Pearl of Great Price... your great reward.

About the Authors

Kim and Mary Andersson are founders of Christ the Rock Ministries and senior leaders of Christ the Rock Fellowship in Anderson, CA. They oversee a ministry school and train prophetic teams, which travel with them to minister strength and encouragement to churches, Bible colleges and conferences, both regionally and internationally. They have four children and two grandchildren.

They are currently writing, a soon to be released book called, "The Body Builders"... the second in the series called, Night Vision ©. The Night Vision © series is based on the concept, "A picture is worth a thousand words." Using dreams as modern day parables, the authors explore the ways that God often instructs us in the night time hours. As the Spirit is being poured out on all flesh in these last days, it will become increasingly more important, for believers to understand and interpret God's communication with us through dreams and visions.

Other books available through their ministry:

"For Freedom's Sake" is a study book designed to help the believer obtain freedom from the wounds of the soul. Jesus' desire is for us to be "free indeed." This book will take you on a personal road of discovery, as you learn how to rule over, and break free from the issues that control you. It's an excellent tool for deliverance preparation and follow-up.

"Scrupulous Conformity" is the first book in the series Night Vision ©. Based on the imagery of a vivid dream about the religious spirit; this modern day parable will bring to light the issues in our lives that make room for the religious spirit to operate. The reader will learn how to identify the nature of religion, its hidden agenda, and how to remain free from its control.

For more information, visit us at:

www.christ-the-rock.org

or

http://www.myspace.com/ christtherockministries

or

www.christtherockministries.blogspot.com

Write to us at:
Christ the Rock Ministries
P.O. Box 1474
Anderson, CA 96007

For Bulk orders:

Please Contact

Accent Digital Publishing

2932 Churn Creek Rd

Redding, CA 96002

Email: orders@accentdigitalpublishing.com

(530) 223-0202